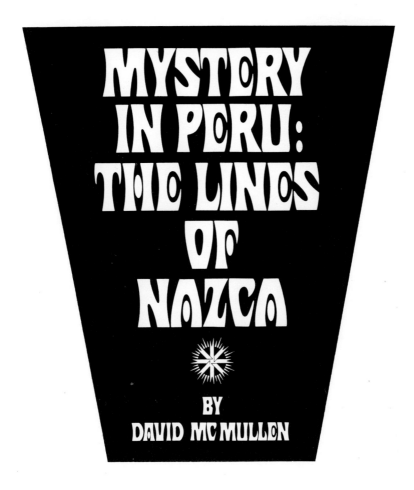

MYSTERY IN PERU: THE LINES OF NAZCA

BY
DAVID MCMULLEN

A

cpi

Book

From

RAINTREE CHILDRENS BOOKS
Milwaukee • Toronto • Melbourne • London

7 8 9 10 11 12   89 88 87 86 85

Library of Congress Number: 77-10456

Art and Photo Credits

Cover illustrations, Lynn Sweat.
Photos on pages 7, 8, 10, 13, 14, 16, 19, 21, 33, 37, 40, 41, 43, 44, and 46,
The International Explorers Society
Illustration on page 35, Lynn Sweat
All photo research for this book was provided by Roberta Guerrette.
Every effort has been made to trace the ownership of all copyrighted material in
this book and to obtain permission for its use.

Library of Congress Cataloging in Publication Data

McMullen, David W., 1939-
  Mystery in Peru: The LInes of Nazca

  1. Indians of South America—Peru—Nazca—Antiquities—Juvenile
literature. 2. Nazca, Peru—Antiquities—Juvenile literature.
3. Balloon ascensions—Juvenile literature. I. Title.
F342.9.N3M3 985'.2 77-10456

Manufactured in the United States of America.
ISBN 0-8172-1058-X lib. bdg.
ISBN 0-8172-2163-8 softcover

CONTENTS

Chapter

1

SEEING
IS
BELIEVING

You are flying in a small plane off the coast of Peru. The morning is clear and sunny. Darts of light sparkle from the blue Pacific waters below. The pilot turns the plane inland. You are moving toward the hot desert plain of Nazca and a mystery that started 2,000 years ago.

You are in the plane with Jim Woodman, a modern day explorer. Woodman is playing detective. He is searching for the reason an ancient people would have to carve lines and pictures in the sun-baked Nazca soil. "Pictures that only can be seen from the skies," he tells you, "Pictures that have lasted thousands of years and never were meant to be seen from the ground!"

Ancient pictures that only people who fly can see. Why? Certainly there were no airplanes 2,000 years ago! *Or were there?* Jim Woodman worked long and hard to come up with the answer to that question. He never bargained for the adventures he would have in trying to find that answer. Here is your chance to see how Jim Woodman tried to solve the mystery in Peru— *the mystery of the Nazca lines.*

Peru is in northwest South America. The main city in Peru is called Lima. It's quite a modern place, with a population of almost 2,000,000 people. But the lines are located in the little village of Nazca. Nazca is in the "middle of nowhere." Because it is an extremely dry area, with little but stony soil, very few people live there. Those who do, live much the same way their ancestors did hundreds of years ago.

Jim had to take a jet to Lima. There he rented a small Cessna plane to fly to Nazca. It was a long, tiring journey from the United

The lines of Nazca were drawn 2,000 years ago by the Incas.

As you approach the plain, the "runway" comes into view.

States, but his excitement was building. There was something about this wild, hidden place that told him deep, age-old secrets were kept here. Jim knew the lines must be a secret that only a few people on earth could share in this out-of-the-way village. And this secret had been kept from the world for at least 2,000 years!

Woodman wondered if he could unlock the secrets of Nazca. He felt as if someone had sent him a 2,000 year old telegram of drawings and lines. He was now anxious to open that telegram and find out what his ancient friends were trying to tell him.

Jim was impatient as the plane was refueled. A cameraman, along on the trip, was adjusting his special camera. If the lines of Nazca can only be seen from the air, did the early inhabitants of Nazca have airplanes? He quickly put the thought from his mind. People would laugh at such an idea. But the thought of ancient flyers would return to him often. Finally, Woodman was off.

The little plane climbed through the still, crisp air. There wasn't a cloud to be seen in any direction. The pilot headed the plane for the huge, flat desert. As they approached it, Jim Woodman gasped. Down on the edge of the plain, as clear as could be, were two large triangles drawn on the ground. *Were they there to point the way to Nazca?*

Suddenly, a series of lines appeared—great white slashes that could be seen through the dry grass. They went on for as far as the eye could

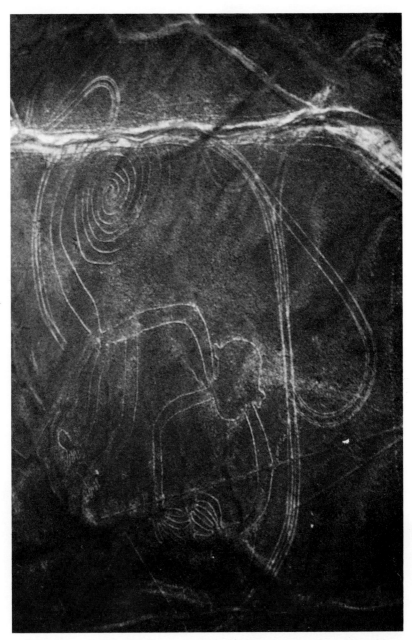

Seen from the air, the lines seem to form pictures, what does this one look like to you?

see. Every now and then they all came together at a point, making a star-like shape. The pilot slowed the plane and moved lower. Woodman's mind was crowded with questions he would go on asking all his life. He looked to the left. His eyes widened, and he grabbed the arm of his photographer. "Look," he cried, "get a picture!"

Gazing up at them from the ground was a design that seemed familiar. Could it be? Were they seeing the outline of a large bird? Yes, it was a bird—a *condor*! The condor was cut into the ground. There was no mistaking its clean, white lines. The condor stared up at them eerily. Jim shivered a little at the thought that it had been looking up into the skies like that for thousands of years!

Woodman suddenly realized that he could not be the first person to look down on these lines of Nazca. He was now certain that the ancient artists had cut these designs into the ground for someone in the air to see. *But who?* Woodman could not shake the feeling that he was on the verge of a great discovery.

As they flew on, they saw more designs—monkeys, spiders, and strange spirals were carved into the ground. The cameraman began to complain. He couldn't take the pictures he wanted from his position inside the plane. He wanted to hang freely over the designs. The pilot landed. The three men climbed out of the little plane. Using thick anchor ropes, they carefully strapped the photographer to the wing.

Jim Woodman walked over to where he had seen one of the lines from the air. But here on the land it seemed to vanish. It looked like a simple path cut into the dry grass that might have been made by wandering animals over the years. Except there were no animals around large enough to make them. Besides, animals aren't artists! The lines he had seen from the air were no accidental paths. They were carefully cut into the earth by people who knew just what they were doing! He'd stake his life on that!

When Woodman was again in the air, he noticed that the smaller lines could be seen only when the plane flew low over the ground. As the little plane—with the cameraman still tied to the wing—climbed higher and higher, the larger lines alone were visible. Different pictures appeared depending upon the height. And all of this had been drawn 2,000 years ago! Woodman would

This ground drawing looks like a hummingbird.

not rest until he learned who was supposed to see these pictures that were made during the days of the ancient Roman Empire.

Higher and higher the Cessna rose into the air. The photographer clicked happily away. Below him, the clear lines and shapes stood out sharply against the reddish land. He didn't seem at all afraid that he was hanging from a plane

The lines of Nazca disappear on land. This terrain shot shows the beginning of one of the giant animals.

hundreds of feet above the earth. Woodman didn't know what to think about first. Would the anchor lines that held his photographer be strong enough?

The plane turned from the land and began to fly toward the sea.

"What's going on?" Jim asked the pilot.
"You'll see!" was all that the pilot would say.
"What did he say?" called the dangling cameraman.
"He said load up with film . . . there's something more to see."

Jim wondered what on earth the pilot had in mind. He got his answer quickly enough. As they swung in toward the land again, they saw a giant branched candlestick cleanly cut into the hillside.

"No one knows what it means . . . or even what it really is," the pilot called over his shoulder. "It stands 840 feet tall, and the first Spaniards to come to this place saw it for miles from the sea."

Woodman couldn't believe his eyes. The drawing stood out as brightly as a beacon.

"It seems to point toward the lines and shapes we were just flying over," Jim replied, thoughtfully.

"Very nearly does," replied the pilot. "It's just a few degrees off. If an ancient pilot had used the candelabra to tell direction, he would have missed the lines of Nazca by many miles."

Jim nodded and smiled. "So this pilot also believes in ancient fliers," Woodman thought. Woodman couldn't shake the idea that it was the people of Nazca who were the fliers rather than some more advanced neighbors.

The Candelabra of the Andes is an 840-foot carved drawing. It is believed that the drawing was used to show direction.

Jim shrugged his shoulders. His thoughts began to take shape. These lines and figures were made by the Incas, people who lived 2,000 years ago and knew how to fly. But how? That was what he decided to find out at all costs.

Just then they all looked down and laughed. Right below them, carved on the side of a rock, was a little Inca figure waving "welcome" to them. They waved back, laughing. But soon they grew quiet. Each man realized that the little figure had been waving that welcome for 2,000 years. Who was the figure supposed to be waving at? Who did the ancient people of Nazca want to welcome?

Were the lines of Nazca the remains of an ancient airport? If so, where were the buildings? Where were the remains of the crafts used for flying? Jim didn't know but he was going to find out.

Chapter

2

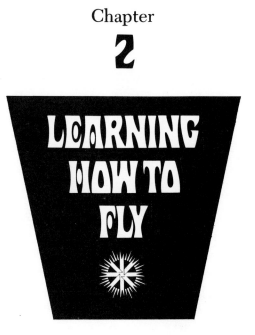

LEARNING HOW TO FLY

Woodman returned to the United States. The first thing he did was to have his photographs developed. And he began long research into the possibility of ancient astronauts and fliers. Woodman found that a man named Von Daniken had flown over the lines of Nazca before he had. Von Daniken believed that spacemen from another planet had landed in Nazca over 2,000 years ago. Woodman found it all very strange and could not accept Von Daniken's ideas.

Were the Nazca lines roads or . . . runways . . . or something else?

When Von Daniken had come to Peru and flown over Nazca, the so-called experts told him that the lines were just old roads. Von Daniken couldn't believe that answer. Why would the ancient Incas have built these straight lines side by side in runway designs? Why did they build roads that stopped suddenly in the middle of nowhere? And why did they build six or eight roads that occasionally crossed each other, forming a star? What's the use of a road that can't take any weight, doesn't go anywhere, and can't be seen from the ground?

Von Daniken decided they couldn't possibly be roads. To him the lines looked just like a modern-day airport. The lines had to be used as some sort of runway. That's why they didn't go anywhere. Runways begin and end. They don't act as roads. Neither do the lines. He also decided that the Incas were not advanced enough to have built an airplane. The only answer, Von Daniken decided, was that spacemen from another planet had used them.

Jim Woodman considered all of Von Daniken's ideas carefully. But he wasn't happy with them. He felt that all the clues just didn't add up to spacemen. What would the condor or the monkey mean to visitors from outer space?

Lines begin, end, and intersect in very specific patterns.

21

All the descriptions he had seen of flying saucers showed them rising straight up as a helicopter might rise. They didn't use runways. Besides, the ground itself couldn't hold the weight of a flying saucer.

Woodman knew there had to be another explanation for what he had seen in Nazca. He was sure that somehow the Incas had learned how to fly; but *how*? He didn't know. The photos of the beautiful designs came back from the lab. The lines stood out clearly and kept reminding him of the unsolved mystery he had uncovered.

One day, while reading a magazine article about a new sport becoming popular in the United States, Jim Woodman found an answer! The sport was *ballooning*—filling a large plastic bag with hot air so that the bag rises into the air like a balloon. Woodman immediately called a friend named Michael who had taken up the new sport.

"How does it work?" asked Jim.

The ballonist explained that a gas flame heats up air which is used to fill up the balloon. The hot air is lighter than the cooler air over the earth. The balloon fills up and, as if it were filled with helium, it floats upward. Special seats, or baskets, are suspended from the balloon to carry people aloft. As the air in the balloon cools, it gets heavier and comes back to earth. Woodman listened—and thought. *Could the ancient Incas have known about ballooning?* Was it possible?

"Look Jim," his friend said, "why don't you come up with me next weekend. I'm going up for a little flight quite near here. You can judge ballooning for yourself."

The following weekend, Jim found himself climbing into a little wicker basket that hung from a red plastic balloon. Michael turned up the heat a little to get more lift. Then he let go of the lines holding the bottom to the ground. Then they were off, sailing up into the air so smoothly that Jim hardly felt any movement at all. Yet, he was flying. The roads appeared like lines drawn on the surface of the earth. Woodman felt his heart leap with joy.

Suddenly, everything started to make sense to Jim Woodman. *Everything* on the ground began to look like designs. The Nazca pictures and lines must have stood out more clearly from the balloon than they did from an airplane. "Of course they did," thought Woodman. "A balloon moves much more slowly."

Woodman's mind was racing now. There are no road maps for the air trip! There are no signposts telling direction! A balloonist just follows the wind. Flying over a modern city, the roads beneath you are your compass. But how could the Incas tell direction? They had no roads and highways to look for! The Incas *had* hot air balloons! The lines of Nazca helped them move about over the plains and find their way back home! That must be it!

But even in his excitement, Woodman knew there was a problem to his theory. Hot air balloons were a fairly recent discovery. What right had he to think that they existed 2,000 years ago? The Incas didn't have light plastics to make the balloon. They had no nylon lines, no light gas containers to heat the air. No, clearly he had a lot of work to do. Did his incredible idea have *any* truth to it?

Stepping out onto the ground again, Jim felt a little sad. For a moment—just a moment—he had flown like a bird. He had followed the lines on the ground from the air. The flight was wonderful. He had an exciting answer to the mystery of Nazca. There were no spacemen on the plains of Nazca. They were ancient balloonists. He was sure of it now. But how could he prove it to the world if he couldn't be sure himself?

Woodman had to prove that his idea was right. But it was going to take some doing.

Chapter

3

THE LEGEND
OF THE
FLYING
INCA BOY

Did you ever look for something and not see it even though it was staring you in the face? Jim Woodman had that problem. He knew what he had to find out, but he didn't know where to look. Then he realized, when you need answers you have to ask questions. And once Woodman knew what question to ask the experts, he was swamped with answers. The question? Was there any proof that the ancient Incas flew in balloons?

The first thing Woodman was shown were many pieces of ancient pottery from Peru picturing the Incas in flight. At first, all he found were drawings of men with wings. This certainly meant the Incas were interested in flying. Searching further, he found pictures of men sitting in little boat-like baskets under what looked like balloons. This was exciting. He *was* on the right track!

Woodman also learned that, in some remote tribes, priests still used little model balloons lifted by hot air to send up prayers to the gods. Some tribes had been doing this for thousands of years. How could that be? The hot air balloon was supposedly invented by a Frenchman in 1800! Or so it was supposed to have been! That bit of history turned out to be wrong.

Woodman found evidence that a Peruvian priest called Bartolomeu had made a trip in a hot air balloon 100 years before the Frenchman's invention! In 1709, the priest based the design of his balloon on the ideas and teachings of ancient Inca tribes. Now Woodman knew there really had been hot air ballooning many years before anyone in Europe had even thought of such an idea. But that didn't yet mean that the ancient Incas actually flew in balloons. Woodman now had to hear more about *Antarqui*, the "Flying Inca Boy."

The legend of the "Flying Inca Boy" told a story of the wars between the Incas and the Mayans (a tribe of people who lived to the north of Peru and as far away as Mexico). The Incas sent up a "Flying Boy." His job was to fly over the enemy's lines to report on their location and the direction from which they would attack. The legend simply says that Antarqui, the boy chosen for this daring mission, simply *hung* over the enemy lines in some sort of flying machine.

Was Antarqui flying in a balloon? We can't tell. It is hard to tell from a legend what's fact or fiction. Certainly the description of his "hanging over the enemy" did sound like balloon flying. That Antarqui would be a boy also made sense. The lighter the person in the balloon, the longer the flight could be.

Can you imagine the sight of Antarqui flying over the enemy's lines? No one could shoot at him or his balloon since spears and arrows were the only weapons used at the time.

By now Jim Woodman had little doubt that the Incas flew in hot air balloons. One question

Antarqui, "The Flying Inca Boy," may be a clue in the mystery of the ancient fliers.

was left unanswered. Did the Incas have the materials to make a balloon that could fly? Woodman set out to find the answer. What kinds of linen and cloth did the Incas have 2,000 years ago? What did the ancient Incas use for rope? He decided to return to Nazca. But could he find evidence of the materials used in ancient times?

When Woodman reached Nazca he ran into some unexpected luck. He met an old grave robber. By this time, word had spread about the "crazy American" who believed that the Incas flew 2,000 years ago in balloons. Everyone knew he was looking for samples of very old cloth. And that's just what the grave robber had waiting for him—strips of colored, woven fabric.

"How old are these?" Jim asked the old man.

"About 1,500 years old . . . They are pretty aren't they?"

Woodman agreed that they were. But that is not what interested him. He was looking at the tight weave of the fabric, not the pretty colors. The material was in almost perfect condition!

"This is great," he said, "but do you know of any plain cloth—like ordinary cloth sheets? And where did you get this from anyway? How come it's so perfectly preserved?" The old man could only scratch his head. His friends had been right. This American was indeed a little crazy. "Why would Woodman need plain cloth?" the old man puzzled. It fetched no money at all. "Ah," he sighed. These things were too hard for him to understand. "Plenty . . . plenty of plain cloth. It is lying all over the place for anyone to take. It is worth nothing," the old man finally answered.

"Where?" Woodman asked excitedly. "Can you take me there?"

"In the graves, of course," the old man answered. "Where we get all such things. I will take you. Come."

So Woodman found himself plodding along over the dry ground near the plains of Nazca. And what he found amazed him. The entire area was one giant graveyard! Wherever he looked, there were graves—thousands and thousands of them. Most had been broken into by greedy grave robbers looking for buried jewelry and pottery they could sell. Even Woodman had now joined the ranks of the grave robbers. Wasn't he about to do the same thing?

In this field of graves, Woodman had the ee-rie feeling that ancient Inca warriors were reaching out to tell him about their past. He shivered at the thought. But the old man was unmoved. He went about his job of searching through old skulls and bones.

Gradually, a small pile of clean white fabric, in almost perfect condition, began to grow. The dry air of Nazca kept things from falling apart. Even though the old man couldn't understand what this American wanted, he kept digging. But was this the cloth used to make balloons?

Jim decided to ask the old man what he thought about the lines of Nazca. After all, the mysterious lines and pictures were drawn in the old man's own backyard! The old grave robber again scratched his head and thought for a moment. He said there had been some talk of great birds and spiders drawn on the ground. But, personally, he doubted it. He had never seen any such things himself. And he had lived in Nazca all his life! To him, there were no lines and no pictures carved in the ground. The old grave robber suspected that it was all a story to bring tourists to Nazca. Jim Woodman couldn't believe his ears!

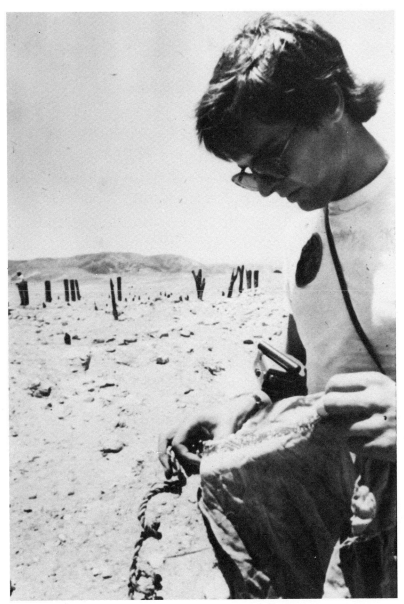

Jim Woodman snapped a picture of his associate, Julian Knott,
examining 2,000 year old cloth in a graveyard in Nazca.

Of course, the old man had never flown in a plane. He was unaware of what was etched in the ground. But he listened to Woodman, not believing a word he was hearing.

Having been paid for his work, the old man left. Woodman went home with the pieces of cloth he had wanted. Now, with all these 2,000 year old jigsaw pieces in hand, Woodman was left with putting the whole puzzle together. A plan came to mind. He was going to build a hot air balloon using only what he thought the Incas could have used. And that included these scraps of cloth. Woodman planned to fly over Nazca as he felt the Incas did 2,000 years before!

Chapter

4

THE FLIGHT OF THE CONDOR

The time had come for Woodman to again ask his friend, the balloonist, for some help. He really needed the help of those who had built his friend's balloon. Of course, by now they had all heard of his theories about flying over the plains of Nazca. Many balloon builders were only too eager to help in such an exciting moment.

Two top balloon engineers took Woodman's pieces of cloth and tested them. What they found was astonishing. The cloth seemed to be stronger than most modern cloths made on today's machines. Also, the Nazca cloth had a tighter weave than any cloth made on a machine.

But why did the Incas create such a tight cloth? Woodman found the answer. It seemed that the waters off the coast of Peru were filled with fish, particularly anchovies. The ancient fishermen had to develop special cloths and spin special lines to catch these tiny fish. Imagine— the Inca weavers made stronger material than almost anything produced on modern weaving machines! The experts felt this cloth very well *could* have been used to make balloons.

Woodman was not ready to build his *Inca* balloon. He and a group from an organization called the *Explorers* set out to prove the Incas could have flown in balloons 2,000 years ago. The Explorers are a group of people interested in finding solutions for great unsolved mysteries. They have uncovered scientific and historical facts that have changed many history books.

Woodman and the Explorers conducted experiments to see what shape the Inca balloons could have been. Helpful in the Explorers' investigation was Dr. Maria Reiche, one of the first Nazca experts. They found that the great balloon was not round like a ball but more like an upside-down pyramid. Huge pieces of cloth

Dr. Maria Reiche joins Explorer investigators Julian Knott and Jim Woodman in the Nazca Valley.

formed the sides of the "pyramid." Beginning at the center, they sewed the pieces together, working their way out. This gave the cloth balloon a spiral shape.

Jim Woodman remembered the spiral shape very well. It is one of the most common shapes in the drawings on the plains of Nazca. Was it possible that the ancient Incas were leaving a plan? Were they teaching future generations how to build their "magical" flying machines? Who knows? But Woodman certainly was now finding a lot more clues in the Nazca lines than when he first saw them.

Finally, the time came for Woodman and the Explorers to try the great balloon. It was made of modern cloth that was very similar to the cloth found in the Nazca graves. Every material used to build the new balloon was made as closely as possible to what the people of ancient Nazca would have used in their time. For example, the new balloon carried nothing made of metal. Woodman used pieces of wood and ropes tied in knots for all the rigging. Even the basket that was placed under the huge balloon was made by hand. It was made in the shape of a small reed boat, a shape used 2,000 years ago. The boat-like basket is called a *gondola*. The passengers would ride in this gondola.

Woodman's group had a funny accident when the little gondola was being made. They had found a little man living way up in the Andes Mountains who still had the skills to build the boat-shaped basket. Woodman wanted the gondola large enough to hold two people. He asked the old man to build it. When they came back for the gondola, the group found that the basket was very small. Why hadn't the builder followed directions?

Then Woodman realized what had happened. The man *had* built it for two men—for two men *his* size. The builder stood less than five feet tall. Jim and his friend would be the two balloonists in this gondola. Both men were six feet tall! Woodman and his friend finally had to ride in the boat-shaped gondola with their feet dangling over the sides. It made a funny sight— they looked as if they were riding horses through the air.

When everything was ready, Woodman and the Explorers went to the Nazca Valley. To the people of Nazca, they must have been a strange sight carrying their ancient, funny-shaped balloon. When they arrived, the first thing the ballooning experts said was: "This place is perfect for ballooning . . . there probably isn't a more perfect place for it in the whole world." Jim just smiled. The experts were only confirming his ideas. The plains of Nazca *were* indeed ideal for ballooning.

The first thing the Explorers had to do was "smoke the balloon." They passed smoke through and around the cloth balloon. Without "smoking," the cloth couldn't hold hot air. There were too many holes in it. These holes had to be filled with smoke and soot particles.

The test balloon was launched by the Explorers to see if a balloon would stay in the air.

Next, the Explorers dug a great pit to hold a great wood fire. They bored a small tunnel that would draw fire and smoke to the open-end of the balloon. The heat from an enormous bonfire of dry wood soon went pouring through the tunnel and into the balloon. The tunnel walls kept sparks from getting into the balloon. After all this work no one wanted to risk an accidental fire. Gradually, the balloon inflated with hot air and began to lift itself off the desert floor.

The *Condor* balloon, lit by fires, makes a beautiful picture on the Nazca Valley.

Less and less smoke escaped through the tiny holes in the cloth as the balloon filled up with hot air and gases. Before long, Woodman and the Explorers faced a balloon that stood as high as a four-story building.

Jim had named the balloon the *Condor*, for the huge birds drawn on the Nazca plain. A picture of the condor was drawn on the side of the balloon. The *Condor* also carried drawings of a sun and a spiral.

People were placed all around the *Condor* hanging onto ropes to keep the huge bag of hot air on the ground. It wasn't easy! At one point, the balloon unexpectedly climbed up into the sky and then dropped onto the desert floor about half a mile away. The *Condor* had taken its first flight, much to the surprise of those trying to hold her down! Woodman and the Explorers scrambled to get back their precious, runaway balloon. When it was back in place, they all had a good laugh. And the accident did prove one thing—their balloon *could* fly! The problem would not be getting it into the air but keeping it on the ground.

Once again, heat from the fire was tunneled into the balloon. The *Condor* rose and blos-

It took many men to anchor the balloon as it was lifted in the air.

somed, spreading its cloth walls into the clear,
calm Peruvian air. The ancient Incas would have
been proud of this flying ship! By this time, the
fire was very large. It had made a large, dark cra-
ter in the floor of the desert. Another clue for
Jim Woodman! He had seen craters like this one
before.

The fire hole began to look more and more like something Woodman had found all over the plains of Nazca. These craters had been a mystery to him when he had first seen them. At the end of many of the Nazca lines were large burned out pits. Had similar hot fires been burned 2,000 years before to fill balloons? No one knows. But it certainly was an interesting new clue.

Was this Inca burn pit used for ballooning or as part of burial ceremonies?

44

Woodman began to piece together his clues.
- the legend of the "Flying Inca Boy"
- the dark pits on the desert floor
- the perfectly still Peruvian desert air, ideal for ballooning
- the strong, white ancient cloth

All he needed now was the balloon flight itself. Jim and his balloonist climbed aboard. It was now or never—success or failure. It was their moment of truth! And then everything happened so quickly. One moment they were straddling the little gondola, and the next they were rising off the ground into the sky.

The *Condor* was flying! Woodman's dream had come true! The ground slipped away from him so quietly, he hardly noticed they had risen. Soon they were looking down from a height of hundreds of feet. The lines of Nazca stood out so clearly it took his breath away. *It had all been worth it!*

The straight lines of Nazca alone could not have told an ancient balloonist enough about flight direction and position. At these heights hot air from the ground rushed up to meet the higher, cooler air, creating small winds. A floating balloon pushed by these winds, could be carried fast and far across the plain. Pictures added to the

Woodman's dream had come true. The *Condor* flew over Nazca.

lines would give the flyer a clearer understanding of where he was.

Woodman was sure now that he was proving the theory he had worked so long to put together. Flying in the *Condor,* he was repeating the flight of ancient baloonists who gazed down at these Nazca lines some 2,000 years ago!

Woodman's flight was over all too soon. He and the balloonist scrambled out of the little gondola. The balloon had been a total success. Everyone cheered. As the group returned to the village, they passed the old grave robber. He shook his head sadly. Had the sun gotten to them? Whoever heard of such a thing? Trying to *fly* over the plain of Nazca. The old man's thoughts turned back to what was really important. Which grave would he rob tomorrow? He promptly dismissed those "bird men" from America who had invaded his quiet village.

Today, the mystery in Peru remains unsolved. No one can prove a theory for the lines at Nazca. Bright and daring adventurers like Erich Von Daniken and Maria Reiche, who has studied Nazca for years continue to investigate. And their debate goes on. Was the Nazca Plain a landing field for ancient astronauts? Did these visitors from other worlds befriend the Incas? Were the Nazca lines drawn to identify the area for other astronauts in flights that came later?

In the book, "The Case of the Ancient Astronauts," by I.J. Gallagher, we are given some evidence of ancient space visitors. Ancient Inca drawings are shown to picture rockets and space machines. Von Daniken's own book, "Chariots of the Gods," describes the Nazca lines as being drawn by people who lived in the Andes even before the Incas. His view of the lines gave him the feeling he was looking at a pre-historic airfield.

There are other theories, of course. Many archaeologists feel the Nazca lines were roads. Others claim the lines and drawings are religious in nature. There is the theory that the lines form some kind of calendar, since it is clear that whoever had the lines drawn used a knowledge of astronomy in the plan. And there is the Woodman theory of ancient balloonists.

Did the Incas fly in balloons 2,000 years ago? Woodman thinks so. Many, many others doubt that he is right. You have read his evidence. You will want to read more about the Nazca mystery before you decide why the ancient lines were drawn. Finally, the answer will be up to *you*.